ANIMALS IN OUR CARE
RABBITS

Written by Alex Hall

American adaptation copyright © 2026 by North Star Editions, Mendota Heights, MN 55120. All rights reserved. No part of this book may be reproduced or utilized in any form or by any means without written permission from the publisher.

Rabbits © 2024 BookLife Publishing
This edition is published by arrangement with BookLife Publishing

sales@northstareditions.com | 888-417-0195

Library of Congress Control Number:
2024952950

ISBN
978-1-952455-38-4 (library bound)
978-1-952455-94-0 (paperback)
978-1-952455-74-2 (epub)
978-1-952455-58-2 (hosted ebook)

Printed in the United States of America
Mankato, MN
092025

Written by:
Alex Hall

Edited by:
Elise Carraway

Designed by:
Ker Ker Lee

All facts, statistics, web addresses and URLs in this book were verified as valid and accurate at time of writing. No responsibility for any changes to external websites or references can be accepted by either the author or publisher.

Photo Credits – Images courtesy of Shutterstock.com, unless otherwise stated.

Cover – xjrshimada, Csaba Vanyi, yykkaa, Badun, Kingarion, Mary Swift, cynoclub, Arlee.P, Jim Cumming, photomaster, DibasUA. 2–3 – AN Photographer2463, JIANG HONGYAN. 4–5 – Dorottya Mathe, Arlee.P, Oleksandr Lytvynenko. 6–7 – Arlee.P, photomaster, Eric Isselee, J Curtis. 8–9 – Eric Isselee, Tonia Kraakman, Roselynne. 10–11 – Arlee.P. 12–13 – Eric Isselee, GPPets, Dorottya Mathe, IrinaK, StockPhotosArt, Sujatha Vempaty, Owl_photographer. 14–15 – Tatiana's Camera, Anita Ng. 16–17 – photomaster, Peyker. 18–19 – Peyker, nicepix. 20–21 – Try_my_best, KanphotoSS, AN Photographer2463, New Africa. 22–23 – STUDIO DREAM, Epic Vision, Prostock-studio, Oleksandr Lytvynenko, Arlee.P, Nattaro Ohe.

CONTENTS

Page 4	Rabbits
Page 6	Rabbits and Hares
Page 8	Rabbit Faces
Page 10	Body of a Rabbit
Page 12	Breeds and Colors
Page 14	Caring for Your Rabbit
Page 16	Body Language
Page 18	From Kit to Rabbit
Page 20	Believe It or Not!
Page 22	Are You a Genius Kid?
Page 24	Glossary and Index

Words that look like <u>this</u> can be found in the glossary on page 24.

RABBITS

What do you like about rabbits?

Do you like their big ears or fluffy tails? Maybe you like how they hop across grass.

Many rabbits are domesticated. They are looked after by humans.

Rabbits are part of a group called the Leporidae <u>family</u>.

Rabbits are mammals. Mammals are warm-blooded animals that have a backbone and make milk to feed their young. Rabbits are herbivores. They only eat plants.

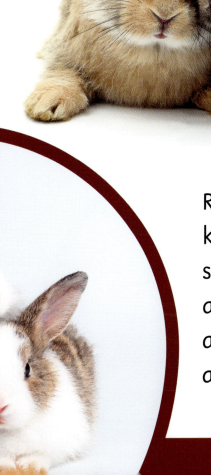

Rabbits are known for being small, cute animals. They are often known as bunnies.

RABBITS AND HARES

The Leporidae family includes rabbits and hares. They are grouped together because of how similar they are to each other.

Rabbit

There are some things that all rabbits and hares have in common. However, there are some key differences, too.

Hare

Rabbits are usually smaller and have shorter ears than hares.

While some rabbits have been domesticated, hares are not domestic animals.

Male rabbits are called bucks. Female rabbits are called does.

DID YOU KNOW?
There is a type of hare called a jackrabbit. How confusing!

RABBIT FACES

Let's look at the face of a rabbit.

Rabbits have eyes on either side of their heads. This lets them see nearly all around them. However, they cannot see beneath their nose.

So rabbits use thick whiskers to feel things below their noses.

Rabbits twitch their noses to help them smell better.

Rabbits have sharp teeth to cut through plants such as grass. Their teeth are always growing. They need to chew a lot to keep their teeth a healthy length.

BODY OF A RABBIT

A rabbit's small tail is called a scut. Rabbits use their scuts to <u>communicate</u> with other rabbits.

Rabbits have strong legs. Their legs let them run and jump long distances.

Rabbits have long ears and excellent hearing. They can turn their ears to find out exactly where a sound is coming from. Large ears also release heat to help rabbits stay cool.

Rabbits have five digits on each foot. Rabbits walk and jump on the tips of their digits.

DID YOU KNOW?
Digits is another word for fingers and toes.

BREEDS AND COLORS

There are many different types of rabbits. These types are known as breeds. Unlike wild animals that change naturally, breeds are controlled and changed by people. There are more than 50 breeds of domestic rabbits.

Angora rabbit

Dutch rabbit

English lop

Lionhead rabbit

Rabbits can be many different colors. They can have <u>unique</u> patterns on their fur.

Many white rabbits have red eyes. These are called ruby-eyed white rabbits.

Blue rabbit

Broken pattern rabbit

DID YOU KNOW?
Sometimes gray animal fur is called blue.

Chocolate rabbit

Black rabbit

13

CARING FOR YOUR RABBIT

Before rabbits were domesticated, they were wild animals. Domesticated rabbits have some of the same natural instincts that wild rabbits have. These instincts help them stay safe.

Wild rabbits live in burrows. Domestic rabbits often enjoy exercising in tunnels and mazes.

14

Wild and domestic rabbits are <u>social</u> animals. They prefer to live with other rabbits. If you have pet rabbits, it is best to have at least two to keep them happy.

Rabbits need lots of hay and grass to eat. They need clean water to drink and a safe shelter.

BODY LANGUAGE

Rabbits often use their feet to communicate. If rabbits are scared, they may kick or thump the ground. Stressed rabbits clench their facial <u>muscles</u>.

Sometimes, angry rabbits stand on their back legs and grunt.

Angry rabbit

Rabbits may show excitement by running around your feet in circles.

If rabbits are happy, they may jump in the air, twist their bodies, and kick their back legs. This is called a binky.

FROM KIT TO RABBIT

Rabbits go through different stages throughout their lives.

Baby rabbits are called kits.

DID YOU KNOW?
Rabbits are born with their eyes closed.

Kits drink milk from their mothers. This milk is very <u>nutritious</u>. They do not need to drink much to stay healthy.

Rabbits become adults from around one to five years old, depending on the breed.

Adult rabbits can have their own young. Female rabbits are usually pregnant for around one month. Each rabbit usually gives birth to around six kits at a time.

BELIEVE IT OR NOT!

Rabbits can jump nearly 35 inches (89 cm) high in a single jump.

Rabbits eat some of their own poop. This poop is different than their normal poop. It is softer and full of the leftover nutrients from their food. It is called cecotropes.

Rabbits do not normally eat carrots. Rabbits should only eat carrots as a treat. Too many carrots can be unhealthy.

Sometimes rabbits purr like cats do. They do this when they are happy and calm.

ARE YOU A GENIUS KID?

You are now full of fascinating facts about rabbits. You are probably excited to share your facts with all your friends. First, let's see if you are really a genius kid.

Check back through the book if you are not sure.

1. Why do rabbits twitch their noses?
2. What are rabbit tails called?
3. What is a binky?

Answers:
1. To smell better. 2. Scuts. 3. A rabbit's happy dance where it jumps in the air, twists its body, and kicks its back legs.

GLOSSARY

communicate to pass information between two or more things

family a way of grouping animals with very similar traits

instincts natural patterns of behaviors in animals

muscles the parts of the body that allow the body to move around

nutritious something with natural substances that plants and animals use to grow and stay healthy

social to do with being in a group or community

unique one of a kind or very rare

INDEX

ears 4, 7, 11
eyes 8, 13, 18
fur 13
hares 6–7
kits 18–19

legs 10, 16–17, 23
noses 8–9, 23
poop 20
scuts 10, 23
tails 4, 10, 23

24